Air
in Action

Library Edition Published 1990

Published by Marshall Cavendish Corporation
147 West Merrick Road
Freeport, Long Island
N.Y. 11520

Printed in Italy by New Interlitho, Milan

© Marshall Cavendish Limited 1989
© Cherrytree Press Limited 1988

Library Edition produced by DPM Services Limited

Library of Congress Cataloging-in-Publication Data

Kerrod, Robin.
    Air in action / by Robin Kerrod: illustrated by Mike Atkinson
and Sarah Atkinson.
      p. cm. — (Secrets of science : 1)
    "A Cherrytree book."
    Includes index
    Summary: A collection of science activities demonstrating the
properties of air.
    1. Air — Experiments — Juvenile literature. [1. Air-Experiments.
2. Experiments.] I. Atkinson, Mike. [1]. II. Atkinson, Sarah, [1].
III. Title. IV. Series: Kerrod, Robin, Secrets of science : 1.
Q161.2.K47 1989
533'.62 — dc20   89-997
                                   CIP
                                   AC

ISBN 1-85435-152-4
ISBN 1-85435-151-6(set)

SECRETS OF SCIENCE

Air in Action

Robin Kerrod

Illustrated by Mike Atkinson
and Sarah Atkinson

MARSHALL CAVENDISH
NEW YORK · LONDON · TORONTO · SYDNEY

Safety First

☐ Ask an adult for permission before you start any experiment, especially if you are using matches or anything hot, sharp, or poisonous.

☐ Don't wear good clothes. Wear old ones or an apron.

☐ If you work on a table, use an old one and protect it with paper or cardboard.

☐ Do water experiments in the sink, on the draining board, or outdoors.

☐ Strike matches away from your body, and make sure they are out before you throw them away.

☐ Make sure candles are standing securely.

☐ Wear oven gloves when handling anything hot.

☐ Be careful when cutting things. Always cut away from your body.

☐ Don't use tin cans with jagged edges. Use those with lids.

☐ Use only safe children's glue, glue sticks, or paste.

☐ **Never** taste chemicals, unless the book tells you to.

☐ Label all bottles and jars containing chemicals, and store them where young children can't get at them – and never in the family's food cupboard.

☐ Never use or play with electricity. It can KILL. Use a battery to create a current if needed.

☐ When you have finished an experiment, put your things away, clean up, and wash your hands.

Contents

Air in Action

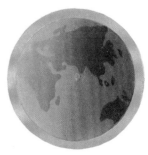

You can't see air. You can't touch air. But you know it's there. You can feel it when you breathe and when the wind blows, and you cannot live without it.

Air surrounds the whole earth. It is made up of a mixture of invisible gases. The gas we use when we breathe is oxygen. It forms about one-fifth of the air. The gas we breathe out is carbon dioxide. It forms only a tiny part of the air, along with several other gases. Nearly all the rest (almost four-fifths) is nitrogen.

Nitrogen

Oxygen

Other gases

Although it is not part of the air, there is always moisture in the air, and there is also dust.

Air keeps us alive. It also helps us in other ways. Air is always in action. When it gets hot, it moves. It rises. Cool air takes its place. This is what makes the wind blow.

Even though we don't notice it, air has weight. It presses down on things, and it holds things up. If you jump from a great height with a parachute, the air holds you up, and it slows your fall so you don't land with a bump.

Seeing Air

Pick up an "empty" glass. Turn it upside down, and push it into a bowl of water. The water doesn't rush into the glass, does it? Air trapped in the glass stops it.

Keep your glass of air upside down in the water, and take another glass full of water. Holding them both under the water, put them together, rim to rim. Now, slowly turn them, so that the air-filled glass is the right way up. Watch the air pour upward into the top glass and force out the water inside.

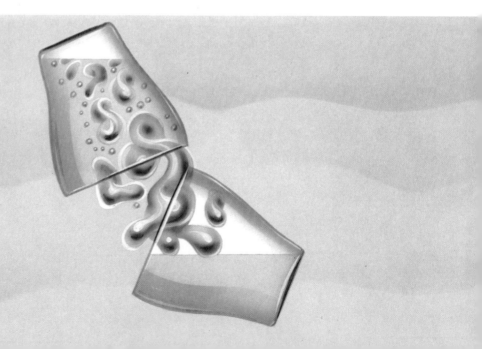

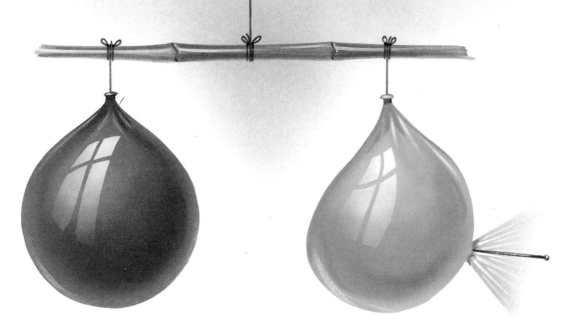

Air is light, but it does have weight.
Blow up two balloons to the same size
(as big as possible). Tie the necks with
string and hang them from the ends of a
thin stick.

Hang the stick from a thread tied in the
middle. Make sure that it is level and
perfectly balanced. Now, prick one of
the balloons with a pin. Watch the other
end of the stick dip. That side is now
heavier, because of the weight of air
inside the unpricked balloon. See what
happens if you prick this balloon, too.

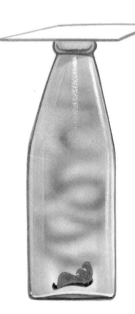

Air on the Move

Air moves around a lot. We feel it as a breeze or wind. Heat makes it move. See what happens to air at different temperatures.

Make a Smoke Bottle

1 You need a bottle, some cardboard, some matches (and permission to use them).

2 Set fire to a piece of cardboard, and drop it into the bottle. Place another piece of cardboard over the top, and watch the bottle fill with smoke.

3 Hold the bottle near a hot radiator, and open the top. Notice which way the smoke goes.

4 Open the refrigerator, and hold your smoke bottle near it. See which way the smoke goes now.

You have seen for yourself that hot air rises and cold air sinks. You can use this fact to make a hot-air balloon.

Make a Hot-air Balloon

1 You need a large plastic bag, a small piece of candle, garden wire, thin wire, and four straight pins.

2 Thread some garden wire around the neck of the bag.

3 Stick the pins into the candle.

4 Use equal lengths of thin wire to hang the candle from the bag.

5 Light the candle, and let the bag fill with hot air. After a while, your balloon should be light enough to fly away.

When the Wind Blows

All the time, great masses of air in the atmosphere are rising (when they get hot) and sinking (when they get cold). This is what causes winds.

Some winds blow because of the difference in temperature between land and sea. The sun heats the land and the sea, but land heats up faster than water does. So, the air above the land gets hot and rises. Cooler air from above the water moves in to take its place, and the result is wind – the brisk breeze that you feel at the seashore.

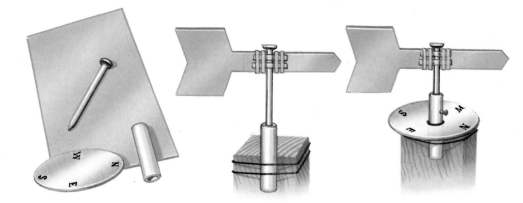

Make a Weather Vane

1 You need heavy cardboard, plastic pipe, strong tape, garden wire, a post, a long nail, and a small screw.

2 Cut out a vane with a point and a tail from cardboard.

3 Cut a circle of cardboard with a hole in the middle, and mark on it the points of the compass (E,W,N,S).

4 Wire the pipe to the post.

5 Place the compass card on top of the post, with N pointing north.

6 Tape the vane to the nail and slip it into the pipe. Insert the screw into the pipe to keep the nail high enough to turn freely.

7 Now, watch your weather vane spin. The arrow will point into the wind.

Make an Anemometer

1 You need four small yogurt cartons, a cork, four small knitting needles, a long nail, two washers, and a post.

2 Make a hole through the middle of the cork, so that the nail can move freely.

3 Stick the needles through the yogurt cartons and into the cork, so that the cartons are all facing the same way.

4 Put the washers on the garden post and hammer the nail through them into the post. The cork should turn freely on the washers. As it spins in the wind, you can tell at a glance how windy it is.

Shrinking and Expanding

Air contracts, or shrinks, when it is cooled, and expands, or gets bigger, when it is heated. Try this trick, and see if you can pick up a bottle without gripping it.

Fill a glass bottle with hot water and leave it in a bowl of hot water for a few minutes. Then, take it out, empty it, and stand it in a bowl of cold water. Place your palm on the neck of the bottle and then lift it. The bottle should lift up with your hand, because the air inside has cooled and contracted. You can use the same idea to stick two glasses together.

Gripping Glasses

1 You need two glass tumblers and a preserving jar rubber ring which fits the rim of the glasses exactly.

2 Put the tumblers in hot water for a few minutes.

3 Take them out and stand one glass upside down on top of the other, with the rubber ring between them.

4 Place the two glasses under cold running water.

5 Now, try to lift off the top tumbler. What happens? You lift them both, don't you?

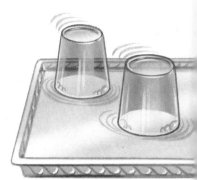

Next time you wash glasses in hot water, place them upside down on a wet tray. Give them a little push, and watch them skid around. They slide because air trapped in the glasses is heating up, expanding and then escaping under the edges. This makes the glasses turn into tiny hovercrafts.

Make a Fountain

1 You need a bottle or jar, water and colored ink, a cork, a straw, some clay, a pin, and a bowl.

2 Fill the bottle half full of cold water colored with ink.

3 Make a hole through the cork, push the straw through it, and seal it tightly with clay.

4 Put the straw and cork into the bottle.

5 Put a little cap of clay on top of the straw, and make a pinhole through it.

6 Now, put the bottle in a bowl of hot water, and wait until the air inside heats up. When it does, it will force the water in the bottle out through the straw in a fountain.

Breaking the Rules

Which is stronger, wood or paper? Try this experiment and see for yourself. You may get a surprise.

A Smashing Trick

1 You need a thin piece of wood, about 18 inches long and 2 inches wide (an old wooden ruler that you don't need will do), two sheets of newspaper, a table, and a hammer.

2 Place the wood on the table so that about a third of it hangs over the edge.

3 Cover the part on the table with two large sheets of newspaper, smoothing the paper so that it is flat.

4 Now, strike the end of the wood sharply with a hammer.

5 What did you expect to happen? The reason the wood broke as it did was that the air was holding it down. The weight of air pressing on the paper prevented the wood from moving. (Four pounds of air presses down on every square inch of newspaper. Can you work out the weight of air pressing down on the whole paper?)

16

You can also crush a can with air. If you want to see how, ask an adult to do this experiment for you. Do not try it yourself.

The Big Crunch

1 You need an adult, an empty can with a screw-on cap, a stove, oven gloves, and a hose or bucket of water.

2 Pour a little cold water into the can.

3 With the cap off the can, boil the water on the stove.

4 When steam comes out of the can, screw on the cap wearing oven gloves. Take the can off the stove and carry it outside. Be careful. It will be very hot.

5 Now, pour cold water over the can, and watch it collapse like a paper bag. What has happened? The cold water has cooled the can and changed the steam inside back to water, greatly lowering the pressure. The higher air pressure outside crushes the can.

Highs and Lows

The pressure of the air in the atmosphere is always changing. We can often tell what kind of weather is coming from the way the air pressure rises or falls. When the pressure rises, it is a sign of good weather. When the pressure falls, it is a bad sign; rain is probably on the way.

We measure air pressure with an instrument called a barometer. You can make one quite simply.

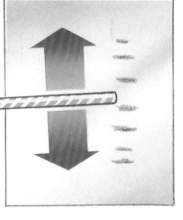

Make a Barometer

1 You need a jar or bottle with a wide mouth, an old balloon, a drinking straw, glue, a piece of cardboard and some string.

2 Stretch a piece of balloon over the neck of the bottle and tie it firmly in place.

3 Glue the end of the straw to the middle of the balloon rubber.

4 Draw a scale from high to low on the cardboard and place it behind the free end of the straw.

5 When the pressure rises, the straw goes up. When it falls, the straw goes down. Can you see why?

18

Make a pile of heavy books, and then try to blow them down. No matter how hard you try, you will not be able to shift them. But there is a way that you can blow them down – if you are cunning.

The trick is to place the pile of books on a large plastic bag. Then blow into the bag. After just a few puffs, the books will start tumbling down. The bag spreads the pressure of your breath over a large area, making a large force, which knocks over the books.

Taking the Plunger

1 You need two kitchen plungers (the kind used to unblock sinks, with a rubber "bell" at the end of a handle), some soapy water and a friend.

2 Thoroughly wet the plungers in water containing a little detergent.

3 Carefully push the ends of the bells together so that you force out most of the air trapped between them.

4 Now, try to pull them apart. Can you do it? If not, ask a friend to pull one while you pull the other.

5 The reason it is so difficult is because you are battling against air pressure. There is hardly any air left inside the bells, so the pressure of the air outside keeps them pushed together.

If you have a table tennis ball and a vacuum cleaner that can blow as well as suck, you can demonstrate another air-pressure trick. But before you start, hang up a pair of apples and try to blow them apart. What happens?

Now, set your vacuum cleaner blowing, with the tube upright. Place the table tennis ball in the middle of the airstream, and take your hand away. You would expect the ball to be blown away, but it isn't, is it? It is trapped in the air. This is because the air is traveling fast. When air goes faster, its pressure falls. This means that the air around the fast air-stream from the blower is at a higher pressure. It stops the ball from getting out.

That is also why the apples moved together when you tried to blow them apart!

Suction and See

When air goes faster, its pressure falls. Because of this, you can make a spray. Place a short straw in a bottle filled with water, and hold it in place with your hand. Now, blow air over the top of the straw with another straw. A spray of water will come out.

By blowing over the top of the short straw, you have reduced the pressure there. So, water is sucked up and broken up into little drops to make the spray. Perfume and paint sprays work in a similar way.

You have a problem. The water level in your rain barrel is too low for you to reach. All you have is a piece of rubber tube. What do you do?

The answer is simple. You suck the water up — just to start with. Put one end of the tube in the water, and suck the water up through it. Once the water is flowing, you can direct the water into a bucket or anywhere you like, so long as the end of the tube is below the level of the water in the barrel. You have made a siphon. You can make a simple version with a plastic pipe in the sink.

Pump It Up

Pull out the handle of a bicycle pump.
Put your finger over the hole at the
other end, and push the handle in. The
handle will go in some way. This shows
that you can squeeze, or compress, air
into a smaller space. When you do so,
you increase its pressure.

When you pump up a tire, you squeeze
more and more air into it. You
compress the air inside. The air
pressure gradually increases, making
the tire harder. If you open the valve on
the tire, the air shoots out as the
pressure falls, and the tire goes flat.

You can use compressed air to make a sprinkler and a pop-gun.

Make a Sprinkler

1 You need a soft drink bottle with a cap, some modeling clay, and a straw.

2 Fill the bottle half full of water, and screw on the cap.

3 Make a hole in the cap big enough to insert the straw. Seal it tight with clay.

4 Blow through the straw into the bottle. Then, take your head away, and watch the fountain of water shoot out.

Make a Pop-gun

1 You need a plastic detergent bottle and some tissues or modeling clay.

2 For bullets, use little plugs of wet, crumpled tissue or clay.

3 Place them in the nozzle of the bottle.

4 Place the bottle on the ground and stamp on it hard.

5 See how fast the plug flies out of the bottle. Measure how far it goes. Have a contest with a friend.

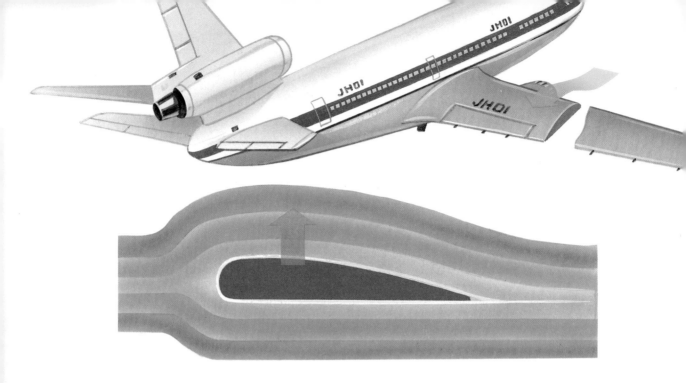

Uplifting

Stand a book upright, and slip a sheet
of paper in the top. Now, blow over it,
and notice that the sheet rises. This is
because air blowing over it (air going
faster) has made the pressure drop.
The pressure underneath is now higher
and lifts the sheet up. This is what
happens when a plane flies. Planes
have specially shaped wings that make
the air go faster over the top. This sets
up a lifting force, which keeps the plane
in the air.

Hang a sheet of paper over a pencil and stick the ends together. Now use a hair dryer (with the heat off) to blow over it. You will find that the paper rises. If you look at the shape that the paper makes, you will see that it is exactly the same as the wing of a plane. A bird's wing has a similar shape.

Planes and birds need not only wings, but tails as well. The tail helps steady their flight through the air. Darts and arrows have "tails" for the same reason. Try throwing a needle at a piece of wood about a yard away, and see how difficult it is to make it stick. Pull a piece of thread through the eye – and see how easy it is. Make sure nobody is in the way!

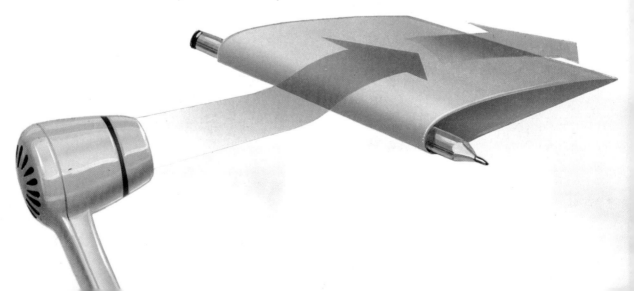

Irresistible Air

Air helps planes to fly, but it slows them down as well. Anything that moves through the air meets resistance. Try running fast, and feel the air against you. If you can't feel it, hold up a tray as you run. You will find it much more difficult.

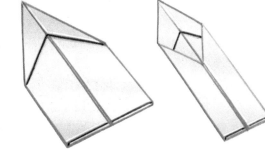

The first planes flew slowly because of their shape. The air rubbed against the wheels and struts. As people learned more about flying, they developed planes with a better shape for flying. They streamlined them, and they flew faster.

Make paper planes for yourself, and see how they fly. See which is the best shape you can make. If you weight the nose of your planes with paper clips, they will fly better.

Air not only slows things down, it also heats things up. Just as rubbing an object with your hand makes it hotter, so rubbing something with air makes it hotter. Lumps of rock from space sometimes fall to earth. As they travel through the atmosphere, they get so hot that they glow. We call them shooting stars, or meteors.

Wet Air

The air contains water. We cannot see it because it is in the form of vapor, or gas. We call the amount of water vapor in air its **humidity**. You can get an idea of the humidity by looking at pine cones. In damp (humid) weather, cones close. In dry weather, they open. You can measure how humid the air is with an instrument called a hygrometer. You can make one if you use your head – or rather, the hairs on your head.

Measure the Weather

1 You need cardboard, a wooden block, thumb tacks, a straight pin, a popsicle stick, tape, and a long hair.

2 Mark a small scale (about one inch) on the cardboard (and decorate it, if you like).

3 Pin the board to the wood so that it stands upright.

4 Trim one end of the popsicle stick into a point. Tie the hair to the pointed end. Put the pin through the other end and into the board opposite your scale.

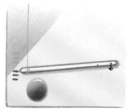

5 Decide whether it is a damp or dry day. Position the point of the stick near the top of the scale if it is wet, and near the bottom if it is dry.

6 Hold the stick in position, then gently stretch the hair in a straight line above the stick and tape it to the board.

7 Watch your hygrometer from day to day, and you will see the stick moving up and down the scale as the weather changes. Hair shrinks in damp weather, and expands when it is dry.

When air containing water vapour rises into the sky, it cools. Little droplets of water form. We see the little droplets as clouds. As more and more droplets build up in the clouds, they bang into each other and join up to make bigger droplets. When they are big enough, the droplets fall as rain – but it takes hundreds of thousands of cloud droplets to make one rain drop.

When it is very cold, the cloud droplets freeze into crystals and fall as snowdrops.

Index and Glossary